TAN DUN

EIGHT MEMORIES IN WATERCOLOR

for piano solo

1. Missing Moon
2. Staccato Beans
3. Herdboy's Song
4. Blue Nun
5. Red Wilderness
6. Ancient Burial
7. Floating Clouds
8. Sunrain

ED 4186
First Printing: January 2004

ISBN 978-0-634-07379-3

G. SCHIRMER, Inc.

DISTRIBUTED BY

7777 W. BLUEMOUND RD. P.O. BOX 13819 MILWAUKEE, WI 53213

MEMORY ON EIGHT MEMORIES

It was on a New Year's Eve, that we met. New Year bells had just finished ringing when friends asked Lang Lang to play. It would be everyone's good fortune to hear together the first music of the New Year. Lang Lang humbly agreed, and played. Everyone was mesmerized by his performance. I was actually speechless for a long while, but nobody knew why. I was very touched, and couldn't really believe my ears. Lang Lang had played "Floating Clouds," one of my first piano pieces written more than twenty years ago (four years before his birth). Lang Lang's interpretation was as pure as water. It almost felt as though I had written this work for him, although he hadn't been born then. I heard the voice inside of me in his playing; I could smell the earth of my homeland. It is a real gift when a musician can play a piece that inspires me to think about where I came from, where I am going. Lang Lang is a poet and has magical powers: he could tell an unending story. In his storytelling, I hear the voice of the human soul and the silence of nature. I do believe Lang Lang is one of the outstanding pianists of our time.

Eight Memories in Watercolor was written when I left Hunan to study at the Central Conservatory of Music in Beijing. It was my Opus One. The Cultural Revolution had just ended, China just opened its doors, I was immersed in studying Western classical and modern music, but I was also homesick. I longed for the folksongs and savored the memories of my childhood. Therefore, I wrote my first piano work as a diary of longing.

In 2001 Lang Lang told me he wanted to present the complete *Eight Memories in Watercolor* in his concert at Carnegie Hall, for which I am very grateful. I made slight revisions to the work, renaming titles, reordering the pieces, and modifying the overall structure, according to Lang Lang's suggestions.

Tan Dun
March 3, 2003

Eight Memories in Watercolor was premiered by Lang Lang
on April 12, 2003 at the Kennedy Center, Washington, D.C.
and recorded live at his November 7, 2003 Carnegie Hall recital
by Deutsche Grammophon, CD 474 820-2

EIGHT MEMORIES IN WATERCOLOR

1. Missing Moon

Adagio con dolore

TAN DUN
(Op. 1, 1978-1979)

2. Staccato Beans

Allegro Scherzando

mp

(the second time faster)

3. Herdboy's Song

4. Blue Nun

5. Red Wilderness

6. Ancient Burial

Tempo I

7. Floating Clouds

8. Sunrain

14